KAI'S DREAM

SHRI BALA & CHENGNA LIN

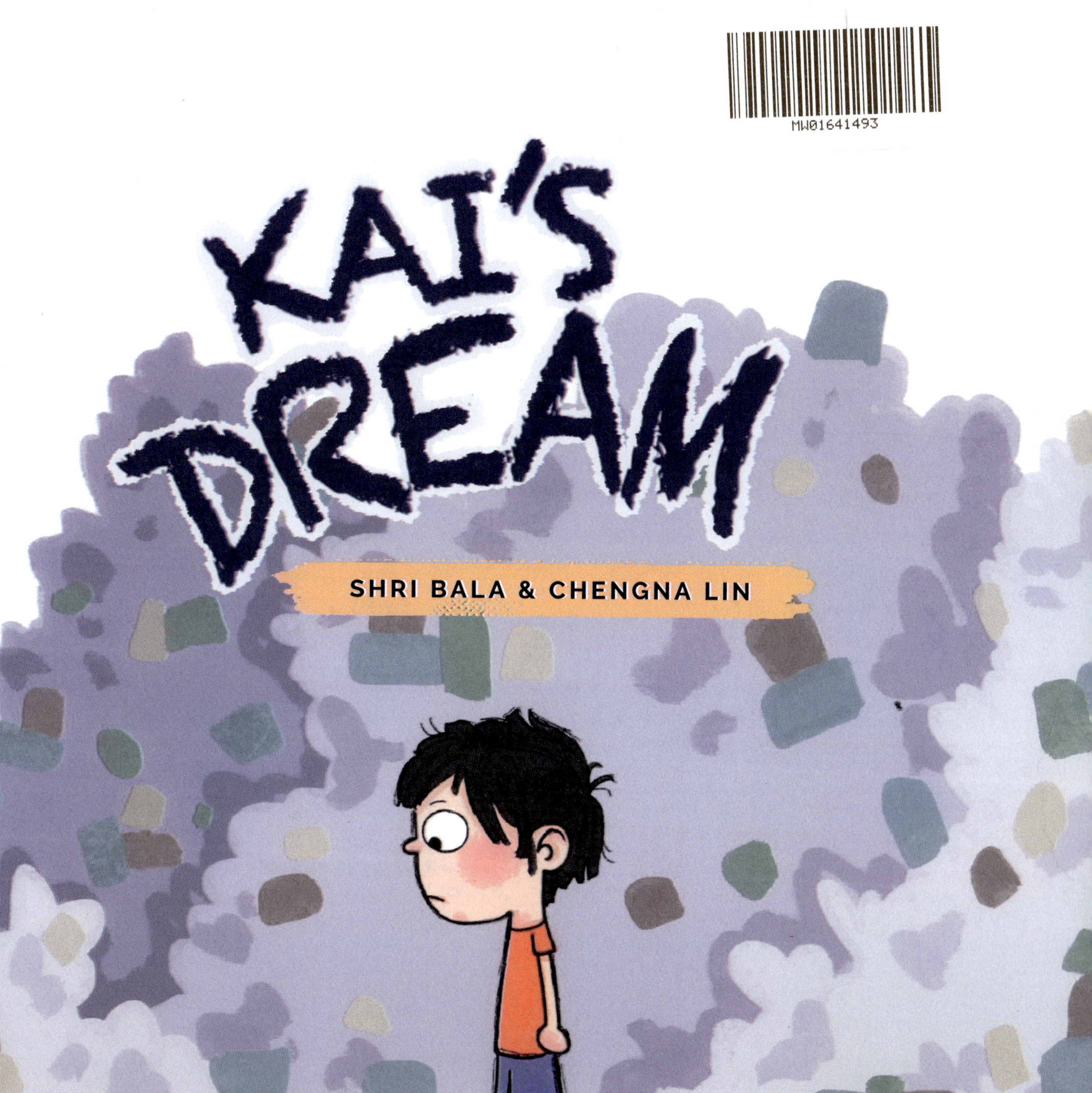

To Hari,

You are the Kai that I aspire to be every day. You will change the world and I hope I can do it with you. Thank you for making me cry, laugh, and smile every day.

-SB

To my Amie Do,

I can never describe how lucky I am to have a friend like you. No matter what I am going through, you are always there. I love you. Thank you for everything.

-CL

SHRI BALA & CHENGNA LIN

Kai is in class.

Ms. Loanny talks about how everyone could help make the planet healthy, but Kai is uninterested.

His eyelids drooped...
and soon he was fast asleep.

As Kai closed his eyes, he felt himself being whisked away. Something magical happened...
and he was transported to a different world.

Kai was in the year 2100.

As Kai looked up, he saw towering buildings
that hid the blue sky.

Far away from Kai, the tall skyscrapers are difficult to see through the dusty fog.

As Kai looks around, everyone around Kai wears a mask that covers their faces.

As Kai looks down, there are little glowing robots everywhere.
They had screens and buttons on them, whirring and buzzing as they moved.

The sounds of wrooms, buzzes, and beeps filled the air from self-driving cars that drove around Kai.

Kai walked over a bridge and noticed the river below was filled with trash: car tires, shopping bags, and plastic bottles

This new world he was in was nothing like the one Kai knew and loved.
Kai felt a pang of sadness and wanted to go back to his world.

Just then, a small robot with friendly eyes rolled up to him.

"Are you okay?" the robot asked Kai.

"Where are we? I want to go home. I do not like it here." Kai says.

"This is the Year 2100. Many years ago, humans did not take care of the Earth. Now, this is what the world looks like." the robot replied.

Kai's heart sank. He wanted to help make
this world beautiful again. He wanted this
world to look like the one he knew.

Just then, Kai heard a familiar sound—his school bell ringing.

Kai opened his eyes and found himself back in his classroom.

"Kai, are you alright?" Ms. Loanny asked in a hushed voice.

But before Kai could answer Ms. Loanny, a piece of paper taped on the blackboard caught his eye.

On the board was an image of the world Kai had just visited.

"That is the year 2100. It is what our world could become in a few years," Ms. Loanny said, noticing Kai's interest.

Kai decided he would help prevent the world from becoming like the one in his dream.

From that day on, Kai listened carefully in Ms. Loanny's class, eager to learn all the ways he could help the planet.
Kai knew that even small actions could make a big difference.

SHRI BALA & CHENGNA LIN

Dear Reader,

Our planet is big and beautiful. But right now, it is getting a little sick because of something called climate change. Climate change is when the Earth's temperature gets warmer and it can cause many problems for plants, animals, and even us!

But don't worry, we can do many things to help our planet feel better. We can use less electricity, ride our bicycles to places, plant more trees, and recycle things instead of throwing them away. Every little thing we do makes a big difference!

So let's work together to take care of our planet so that it can stay a happy and healthy home for all of us.

Climate change is one of the greatest problems our planet faces today, and we need everyone, not just Kai, to help solve it.

So, are you ready to help change the world?

KAI'S DREAM

Made in the USA
Middletown, DE
28 May 2024

54989513R00018

KAI'S DREAM

In a world not so different from our own, Kai falls asleep during class and wakes up in the year 2100. The future is not as beautiful and clean as his world, and Kai is determined to help save it. Join Kai on an adventure as he discovers what the future will look like and how he can save it.

Shri Bala is a high school student born and raised in Fairfax, Virginia attending Falls Church High School. Shri is the older sister to her younger brother, Hari. However, she is also a professional adventurer, full-time eater, human geography nerd, and an active constituent of her friend groups. She enjoys getting up in front of large crowds to make them laugh with her witty dad jokes. When Shri is not learning about urban smart-growth policies or vertical gardening, her favorite hobby is fort-building. She loves diagramming structurally accurate pillow forts with Hari. In case you were wondering, Shri's top three bucket list items are to zipline through the Amazon Rainforest, give a speech on biomimicry to Michael Pawlyn, and design a city that surpasses Wakanda in function and form (without the help of vibranium).

Chengna Lin is a high school student born in Fuzhou, China but raised in Fairfax, Virginia. She will graduate from Falls Church High in June 2025. Chengna is the daughter of Chinese immigrants and the oldest child among her three siblings. Chengna is an avid artist, vlogger, foodie, and friend. Art is a big part of her life. Her deep love for art has helped create her self-identify. She enjoys eating out with her friends and trying new cuisines, and now she and Shri are planning to have a three-day Mukbang. She loves her friends and enjoys every moment with them. Realizing how precious memories are, she has recently decided to document every hangout as a self-made vlogger. Chengna is grateful for being the illustrator of this book and for taking the chance to create change in her community through her passion for art and storytelling.

ISBN 9798323487363